5 EASY DUETS

by Carolyn Miller

Dear Student,

Duets offer great musical experiences that you will remember your whole life long. They help you learn to listen, to count, and to interact socially. These equal-part duets have a variety of styles and keys that I hope will help to improve your technique and musicality. Have fun!

Carolyn Miller

ISBN 978-1-4950-0383-7

EXCLUSIVELY DISTRIBUTED BY

WILLIS MUSIC

HAL•LEONARD®
CORPORATION
7777 W. BLUEMOUND RD. P.O. BOX 13819
MILWAUKEE, WISCONSIN 53213

Visit Hal Leonard Online at
www.halleonard.com

PERFORMANCE NOTES BY THE COMPOSER

Clap Your Hands

This duet requires a very steady rhythm and crisp staccato. Make your hand claps loud and strong so they can be heard by the audience. Enjoy the "high five" at the end!

Hopscotch

I remember playing hopscotch as a little girl, hopping on one foot and then on two. The melody starts in the Primo and moves to the Secondo at measure 9. The B *legato* section at measure 17 is the "resting" part, but the game begins again at measure 25. Pay particular attention to the two-note slurs in measures 32-33.

Autumn Waltz

This waltz should be played gracefully and make you feel like dancing. The accompaniment should always be light. Be sure to always know which part is playing the melody. At the key change, imagine a beautiful large ballroom where you are dancing joyfully.

The Penguins

The phrasing in the piece is very important because it describes the movements of penguins walking! The grace notes are really fun to play, and they further help to visualize a comical colony of penguins. (Special note to Primo: Look carefully at the hand placements in measures 17-24.)

The Traveling Caravan

This is the most challenging duet in the book. Practice the five-finger pattern in G Minor as well as with the raised 4th (G-A-B♭-C♯-D). It might help to imagine two caravans traveling side by side on a vast plain with mountains in the distance.

CONTENTS

Clap Your Hands

SECONDO

Play both hands an octave lower.

Carolyn Miller

Clap Your Hands

PRIMO

Play both hands an octave higher.

Carolyn Miller

SECONDO

*High-five your partner
with both hands!*

PRIMO

*High-five your partner
with both hands!*

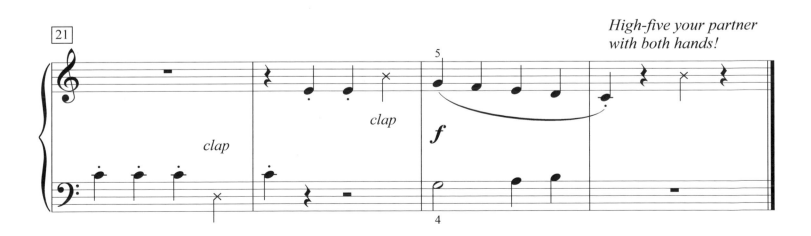

Hopscotch

SECONDO

Play both hands an octave lower.

Carolyn Miller

Hopscotch

PRIMO

Play both hands an octave higher.

Carolyn Miller

Playfully ♩ = 144-160

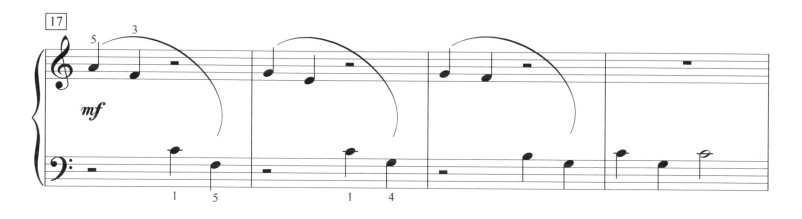

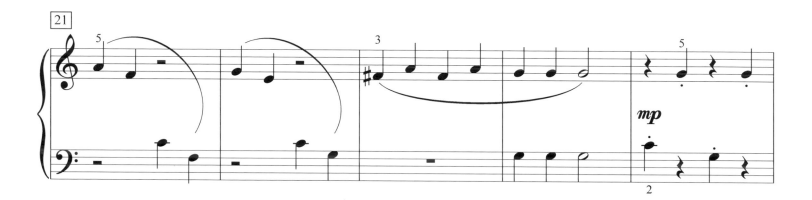

PRIMO

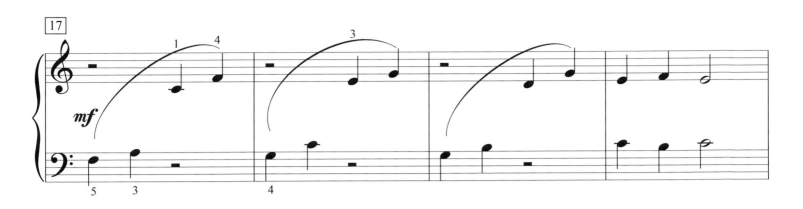

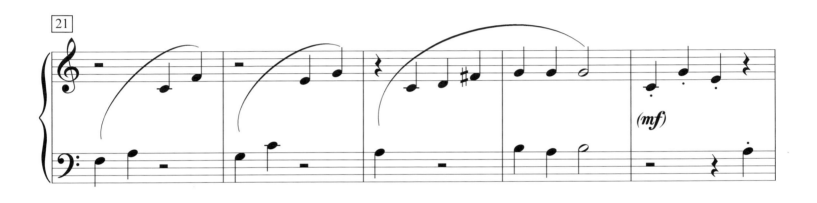

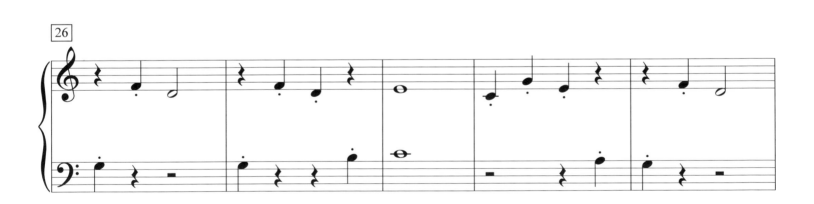

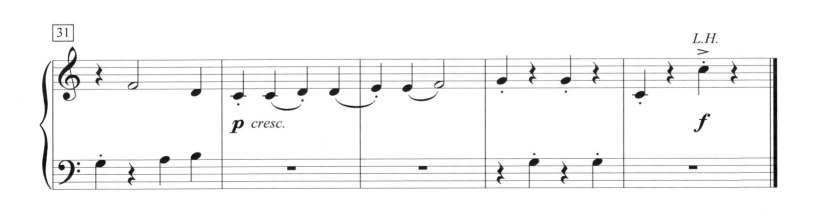

Autumn Waltz

SECONDO

Play both hands an octave lower.

Carolyn Miller

Autumn Waltz

PRIMO

Play both hands an octave higher.

Carolyn Miller

SECONDO

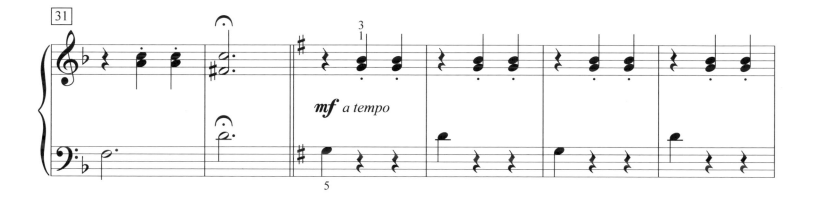

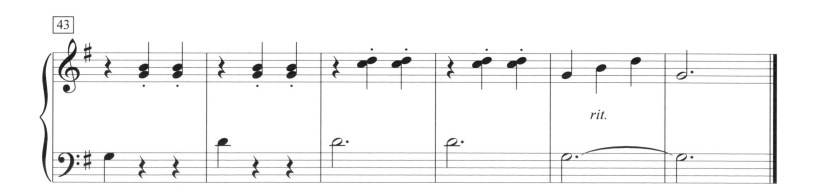

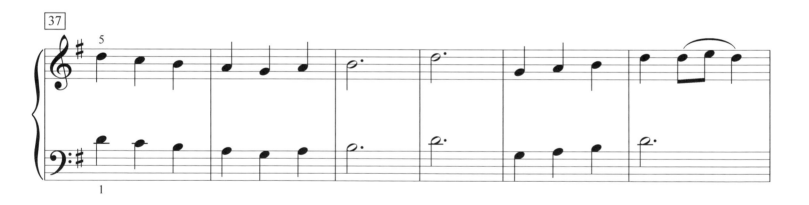

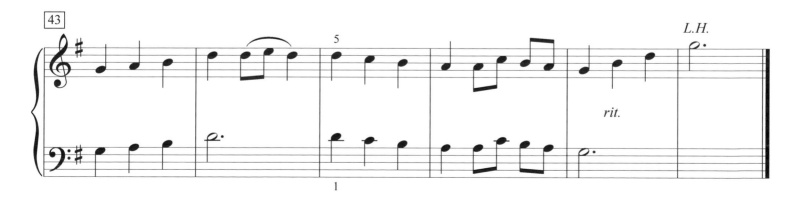

The Penguins

SECONDO

Play both hands an octave lower.

Carolyn Miller

Happily

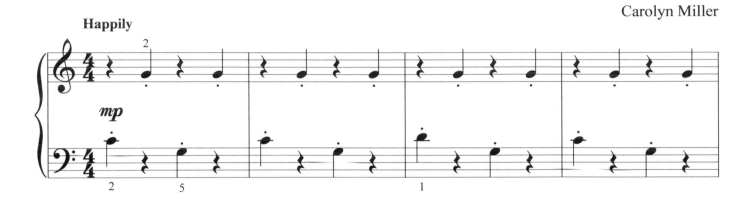

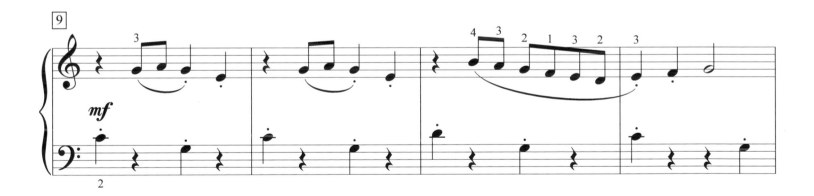

The Penguins

PRIMO

Play both hands an octave higher.

Carolyn Miller

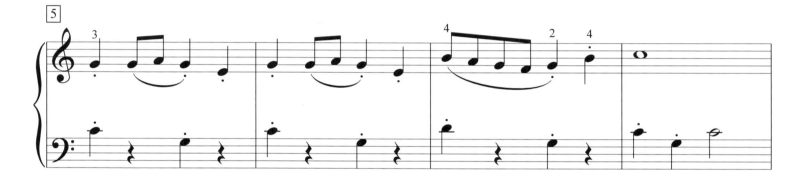

SECONDO

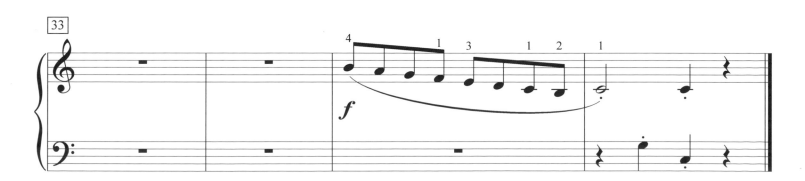

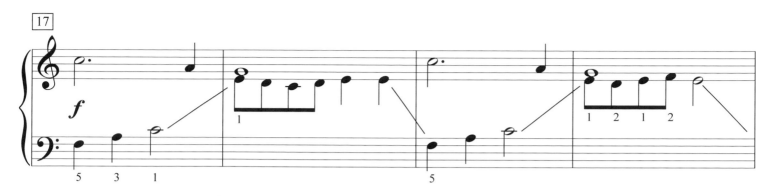

The Traveling Caravan

SECONDO

Play both hands an octave lower.

Carolyn Miller

L.H. detached

The Traveling Caravan

PRIMO

Play both hands an octave higher.

Carolyn Miller

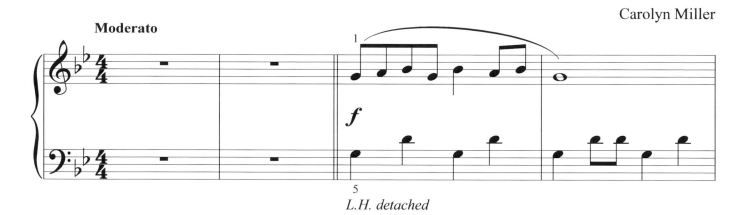

L.H. detached

SECONDO

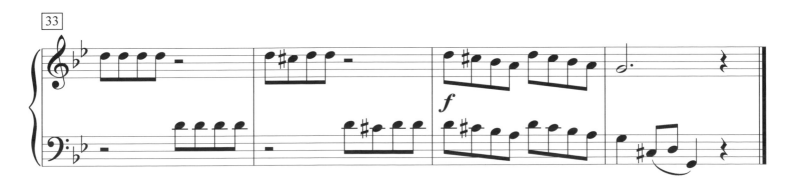

PRIMO

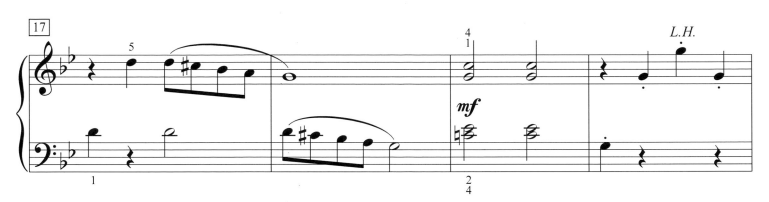

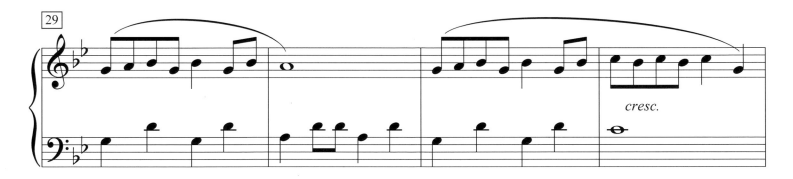

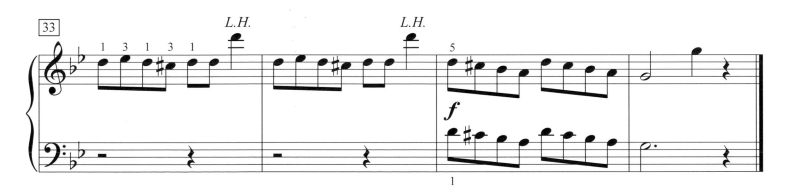

Dynamic Duets
and Exciting Ensembles from Willis Music!

SELECTED COLLECTIONS

00416804 Accent on Duets (MI-LI) /
William Gillock.........................$12.99

00416822 All-American Ragtime Duets
(EI) / *Glenda Austin* $7.99

00416732 Concerto No. 1
for Piano and Strings (MI) (2P, 4H) /
Alexander Peskanov $14.95

00416898 Duets in Color Book 1 (EI-MI) /
Naoko Ikeda $12.99

00406230 First Piano Duets (EE) /
John Thompson series $4.95

00416805 New Orleans Jazz Styles Duets
(EI) / *Gillock, arr. Austin*............$9.99

00416830 Teaching Little Fingers Easy Duets
(EE) / *arr. Miller* $5.99

SELECTED SHEETS

Early Elementary

00406709 Flying (1P, 4H) / *Carolyn Miller* .. $2.50
00406743 Wisteria (1P, 4H) /
Carolyn C. Setliff.........................$2.95

Mid-Elementary

00412289 Andante Theme from
"Surprise Symphony" (1P, 8H) /
Haydn, arr. Bilbro $2.95

00406208 First Jazz (1P, 4H) /
Melody Bober..............................$2.50

00406789 Little Concertino in C (1P, 4H) /
Alexander Peskanov $2.95

Later Elementary

00415178 Changing Places (1P, 4H) /
Edna Mae Burnam $2.95

00406209 Puppy Pranks (1P, 4H) /
Melody Bober..............................$2.50

00416864 Rockin' Ragtime Boogie (1P, 4H) /
Glenda Austin.............................$3.99

00120780 Strollin' (1P, 4H) /
Carolyn Miller.............................$3.99

Early Intermediate

00416754 Bouquet (1P, 4H) / *Naoko Ikeda* $3.95
00113157 Dance in the City (1P, 4H) /
Naoko Ikeda $3.99

00416843 Festive Celebration (1P, 4H) /
Carolyn Miller.............................$3.99

00114960 Fountain in the Rain (1P, 4H) /
William Gillock, arr. Austin........$3.99

00412287 Hungarian Dance No. 5 (1P, 4H) /
Brahms, arr. Wallis.....................$2.95

00416854 A Little Bit of Bach (1P, 4H) /
Glenda Austin $3.99

00416921 Tango in D Minor (IP, 4H) / *Carolyn
Miller*.. $3.99

00416955 Tango Nuevo (1P, 4H) /
Eric Baumgartner $3.99

Mid-Intermediate

00411831 Ave Maria (2P, 4H) /
Bach-Gounod, arr. Hinman........$2.95

00410726 Carmen Overture (1P, 6H) /
Bizet, arr. Sartorio......................$3.95

00404388 Champagne Toccata (2P, 8H) /
William Gillock $3.99

00416762 Country Rag (2P, 4H) /
Alexander Peskanov $4.95

00405212 Dance of the Sugar Plum Fairy /
Tchaikovsky, arr. Gillock $3.99

00416959 Samba Sensation (1P, 4H) /
Glenda Austin.............................$3.99

00405657 Valse Elegante (1P, 4H) /
Glenda Austin $3.95

Later Intermediate

00415223 Concerto Americana (2P, 4H) /
John Thompson $5.95

00405552 España Cañi (1P, 4H) /
Marquina, arr. Gillock $3.95

00405409 March of the Three Kings
(1P, 4H) / *Bizet, arr. Gillock*.......$2.95

Advanced

00411832 Air (2P, 4H) / *Bach,
arr. Hinman* $2.95

00405663 Habañera (1P, 4H) /
Stephen Griebling $2.95

00405299 Jesu, Joy of Man's Desiring
(1P, 4H) / *Bach, arr. Gillock*.......$3.95

00405648 Pavane (1P, 4H) /
Fauré, arr. Carroll......................$2.95

CLOSER LOOK

View sample pages and
hear audio excerpts online at
www.halleonard.com.

WILLIS MUSIC

www.willispianomusic.com

www.facebook.com/willispianomusic

Prices, contents, and availability subject to change without notice.

FOR MORE INFORMATION, SEE YOUR LOCAL MUSIC DEALER,
OR WRITE TO:

HAL•LEONARD®
CORPORATION

7777 W. BLUEMOUND RD. P.O. BOX 13819 MILWAUKEE, WI 53213

0513